## Young Entrepreneurs

# Run Your Own
# Yard-Work Business

### Emma Carlson Berne

**PowerKiDS**
press

New York

Published in 2014 by The Rosen Publishing Group, Inc.
29 East 21st Street, New York, NY 10010

First Edition

Editor: Joanne Randolph
Book Design: Andrew Povolny
Photo Research: Katie Stryker

Photo Credits: Cover Steve Baccon/Digital Vision/Getty Images; p. 4 Digital Vision/ Thinkstock; pp. 5, 6, 26, 28, 29 iStockphoto/Thinkstock; p. 7 Chris Ward/Flickr/Getty Images; p. 9 Rob Marmion/Shutterstock.com; p. 10 Colette3/Shutterstock.com; p. 11 Jupiter Images/Brand X Pictures/Thinkstock; p. 12 Monkey Business Images/Shutterstock.com; p. 13 Purestock/Thinkstock; p. 15 Stockbyte/Thinkstock; p. 16 donald_gruer/E+/Getty Images; p. 17 uniquely india/Getty Images; pp. 18–19 R. Nelson/Flickr/Getty Images; p. 20 STILLFX/Shutterstock.com; p. 21 Blend Images/Shutterstock.com; p. 22 thieury/Shutterstock. com; p. 23 PhotoSGH/Shutterstock.com; pp. 24–25 Mitch York/Photodisc/Getty Images; p. 27 Marc Debnam/Photodisc/Thinkstock; p. 30 Fuse/Thinkstock.

Library of Congress Cataloging-in-Publication Data

Berne, Emma Carlson, author.
Run your own yard-work business / by Emma Carlson Berne. — First edition.
    pages cm. — (Young entrepreneurs)
Includes index.
ISBN 978-1-4777-6125-0 (library binding) — ISBN 978-1-4777-3010-2 (pbk.) — ISBN 978-1-4777-3081-2 (6-pack)
1. Lawns—Juvenile literature. 2. Entrepreneurship–Juvenile literature. 3. Young businesspeople—Juvenile literature. 4. Money-making projects for children—Juvenile literature. I. Title.
SB433.27.B47 2014
635.9'647—dc23
                                        2013034517
Manufactured in the United States of America

CPSIA Compliance Information: Batch #W14PK2: For Further Information contact Rosen Publishing, New York, New York at 1-800-237-9932

# Contents

# Becoming an Entrepreneur

Perhaps you've always assumed that a businessperson has to be an adult. You may have thought that everyone who opens his own company or store is a grown-up, too. Young people can be **entrepreneurs** as well, though. Young people can create small businesses that run just like large ones.

There are many different kinds of businesses. Some people go to work in an office that provides a service to their customers. If an entrepreneur is successful, she may have to hire many employees to run her business.

Some businesses are small, with only one or two workers. Bakeries provide baked goods to people who want them. If there is a demand for baked goods in a certain area, an entrepreneur might open a bakery.

An entrepreneur is any person who notices a need for a product or service and then finds a way to meet that need. This person would create a **business plan**, open the business, manage the business, and, finally, collect the **profits**! In the following chapters, we will learn all about how to create and run your very own business.

# Your Business Idea

Just what kind of business should you create? Look around at your friends and neighbors. What kinds of products or services do they use? Could you provide one of these? What jobs are they doing for themselves that you might be able to do for them? Successful businesses fulfill an existing need or want for their customers.

Most people do not like weeding. This means they very well could be willing to pay you to do it!

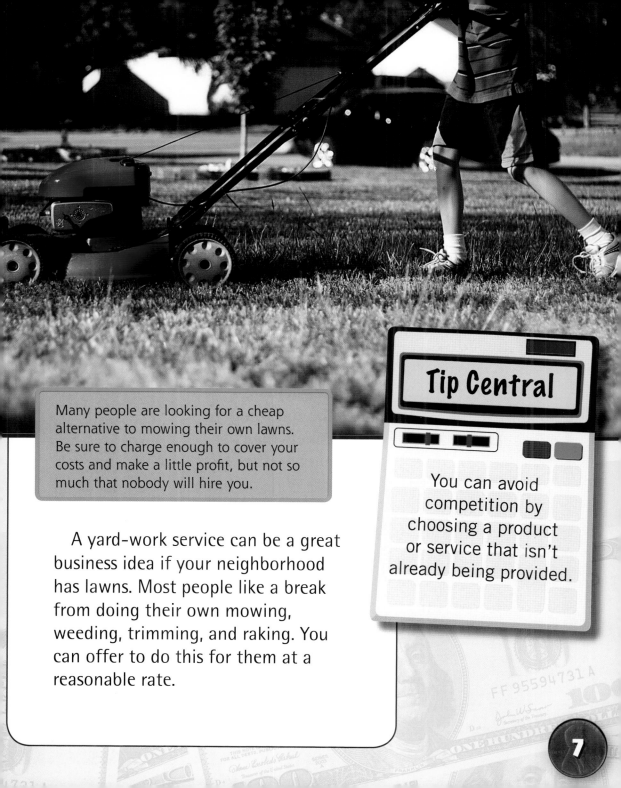

Many people are looking for a cheap alternative to mowing their own lawns. Be sure to charge enough to cover your costs and make a little profit, but not so much that nobody will hire you.

**Tip Central**

You can avoid competition by choosing a product or service that isn't already being provided.

A yard-work service can be a great business idea if your neighborhood has lawns. Most people like a break from doing their own mowing, weeding, trimming, and raking. You can offer to do this for them at a reasonable rate.

# Time to Make a Plan

It's time to make your business plan. Just as the name suggests, a business plan is a detailed outline for starting and running your business. It should answer three questions: where, when, and how?

Your yard-work business is portable, so the "where" is easy. You will go to your customers' yards! When you will schedule clients is a little trickier. Think about the following questions. What will your business hours be? Will you schedule appointments or offer to rake or mow right on the spot? Will you have evening hours? How early can you start in the morning? Are you going to work after school or only on weekends? Have a conversation with your parents about these questions.

A successful business owner is organized. Be sure to write down your ideas, your supply list, and anything else that you do not want to forget.

FF 95594731 A

If a neighbor hires you to plant some flowers in her flowerbeds, you might want to bring a shovel, a spade, a wheelbarrow, and a watering can to water the plants when you are done.

Finally, think about how you will run your business. Yard work requires some basic tools, such as a rake, shovel, hoe, broom, and clippers. You may even want or need a lawn mower and weed whacker. Make a list of tools you will need and think about which you already own or can borrow and which you might need to purchase.

# Tip Central

Consider how you will transport your tools around your neighborhood. You can pile them in a wagon or a wheelbarrow to take them to your appointments within walking distance. If you are providing a mowing service, check with each customer to see if you can use his lawn mower or if you will need to bring your own.

Consider offering a service in which you water people's gardens when they are out of town as part of your business.

# The Business of Budgeting

You can use a computer to help you create your budget. You can also use it to help you get prices for the supplies you need.

Now that you have a business plan, you'll want to think about your **budget**. You have to invest in, or put money into, your business in order to get money out of your business. Of course, eventually, you will want to earn more than you spend. This money is your profit.

To create a budget, write down everything you think you will need to start your yard-work business. Write down even the smallest things, such as gloves or thumbtacks for hanging signs. Put a check next to things you already have. Then circle the items you will need to buy or perhaps rent. These are your expenses. To run a successful business, you want to minimize your expenses. You should spend as little as possible.

## Tip Central

If you do borrow money from your parents, you'll want to draw up a **contract**. This is a written agreement stating how much money you borrowed, when you will pay it back, and whether you will pay it back in one **lump sum** or in **installments**.

Use a calculator to add up your savings. Are you willing to invest what you have saved in your business? Include that amount in your budget.

You will want to include your capital, or the money you are investing, and your costs to get the business started in your budget. If you run short on cash, you will need to borrow money for start-up costs. Don't worry! Most business owners need to borrow some money.

| Expenses | |
|---|---|
| Advertising Supplies | $10.00 |
| Yard Work Supplies (including gloves, spades, shovels, rakes, and more you cannot borrow) | $45.00 |
| **Total** | **$55.00** |

| Capital | |
|---|---|
| Savings | $45.00 |
| **Total** | **$45.00** |

**Expenses – Capital = Total to Borrow**
**$55.00    – $45.00 = $10.00**

You can spend money you have saved, of course, but if you don't have enough, you may need to borrow money. Going into **debt**, probably to your parents, isn't ideal but it's often necessary in order to generate **start-up money**.

Try **estimating** your profits to avoid borrowing too much money. Make an educated guess about how much you think you can make from your business.

Visit your local hardware store to find out the prices for some of the tools and supplies you will need, such as gloves, rakes, and shovels. Include these costs in your budget.

# Awesome Advertising

How will you let customers know that you are now offering yard-work services? How will you convince them to pick your service over others in your neighborhood?

You can make flyers on your home computer and print copies to hang up around town.

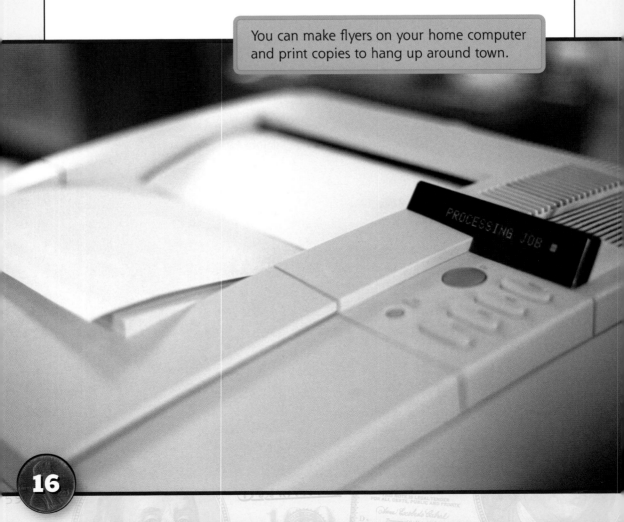

You can make posters using paper, markers, and other art supplies. Try to make your poster stand out. It also needs to be readable and have all the important information on it, though.

Advertising will help you accomplish both of these goals. In your budget, you should have set money aside for advertising supplies. Flyers can be an excellent way to let people know about your business. Be sure to include all the information people will need if they want to hire you. You will want to list exactly what services you offer, such as mowing, raking, bundling sticks, hauling yard waste to the curb, and so on. Your flyer should include what hours you will come out to do yard work, whether you will bring your own tools, and a contact phone number or email address.

Print enough flyers or make enough posters to put into your neighbors' mailboxes. Give some to your friends and ask them to do the same in their neighborhoods.

Advertising is also about attracting customers, not just informing them. Consider making up a catchy name for your business and including a **slogan**, such as "Leave Your Yard Work to Us!" or "Professional Results without Professional Prices."

## Tip Central

If you have your parents' permission, you can also advertise your business using social media. Be sure not to put your personal email or phone number online. Instead, ask people to message you individually if they want to hire you.

# Organizing Your Customers

Monday

Tuesday

1
**4PM MOW THE ALLEN LAWN**

7

8
**4PM WEED AT THE COSTELLOS'**

6
**10AM APPOINTMENT WITH SMITH AND BARTLEY**

14

15

13
**1:30PM APPOINTMENT SMITH AN...**

9

10

16

17

22

23

24

30

09

Write down your appointments on a calendar so you do not forget them.

It's important to be professional when customers start calling. When you answer the phone, always start the same way. Use a cheery greeting that includes the name of your business. Once customers start calling, you will want to keep track of your jobs with a schedule, using a calendar or a notebook planner.

When a call comes in, ask the customer detailed questions about her needs. Then estimate how long that job will take you. You should have already figured out about how many customers or hours of work you can handle each day. Examine your schedule and slot the customer in where you have room.

## Tip Central

To figure out how much you should charge, call a few landscaping companies that do yard work in your area. Explain that you are a kid trying to start your own yard-work business and ask them how much they charge per hour. You will want to charge about half that amount to attract customers.

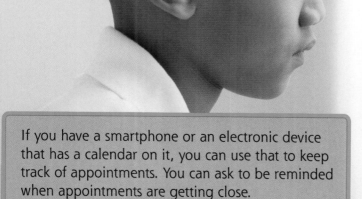

If you have a smartphone or an electronic device that has a calendar on it, you can use that to keep track of appointments. You can ask to be reminded when appointments are getting close.

# Supply Yourself

A yard-work business involves using tools that can be very expensive. It's likely not practical for you to buy tools like rakes, shovels, wheelbarrows, weed whackers, or mowers.

Ask your parents if you can store your tools in the garage, a shed, or a corner of the basement. Keep your supplies neat and tidy so it is easy to find what you need for a job.

You will need many different tools to have a successful yard-work business. A wheelbarrow or a wagon could be a helpful way for you to carry all your tools to your job site.

You can ask to rent or borrow these items from your parents. You can also arrange to use the tools your customers already have.

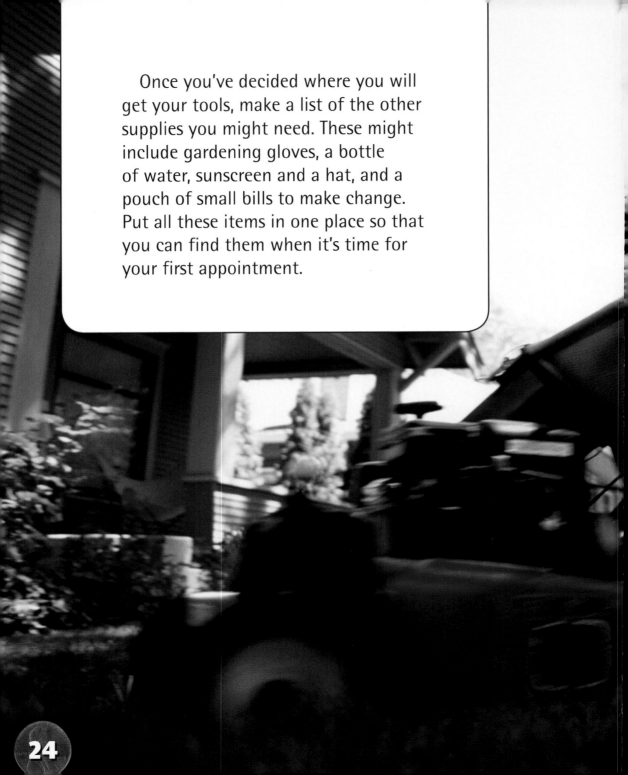

Once you've decided where you will get your tools, make a list of the other supplies you might need. These might include gardening gloves, a bottle of water, sunscreen and a hat, and a pouch of small bills to make change. Put all these items in one place so that you can find them when it's time for your first appointment.

A mower is an important supply, but it is costly and could be hard to get to your job site if it is not close to your home. The person who hires you might let you use his mower, though.

# Getting Down to Business

You've done it! You've made a business plan, set up a budget, and advertised your services. It worked! You're ringing the doorbell of your first customer. Congratulations!

When your customer answers the door, greet her with something like, "Hi! I'm Andy of Andy's Amazing Yard Work. I'm here for our 2:00 appointment."

If you are being hired to weed someone's vegetable garden, be sure you know which plants are the ones she would like to keep. You do not want to weed away your customer's carrots!

# Tip Central

Consider hiring a helper, like a friend. You will need to pay him, but you will be able to work faster and perhaps take on more jobs, increasing your profits in the end.

If many customers want to hire you on the same day, you can save time and fit more work in by hiring a helper. You should be able to do the work twice as fast as you would on your own.

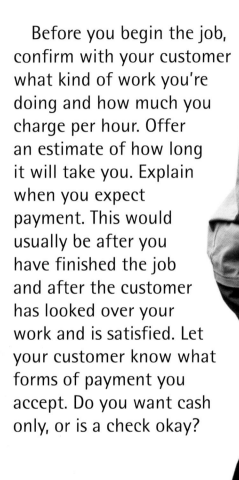

Before you begin the job, confirm with your customer what kind of work you're doing and how much you charge per hour. Offer an estimate of how long it will take you. Explain when you expect payment. This would usually be after you have finished the job and after the customer has looked over your work and is satisfied. Let your customer know what forms of payment you accept. Do you want cash only, or is a check okay?

You may be asked to trim back a customer's bushes. Just be careful when using tools that have sharp edges.

Yard-work businesses can be profitable ones. There are so many different kinds of jobs you can do to help your neighbors out and make money!

Keep a notebook in which you write down each appointment, the type of work done, how many hours you spent, and how much money you made. For instance, you might write, "Mrs. Klein, 23 Maple St., raking and bagging leaves, 3 hours @ $8/hour = $24."

Remember to work hard and always do your best. You want customers to call you again. Repeat customers mean repeat profits. Also, good word of mouth about the work you do will bring you new customers so you can expand your business.

# Are You Ready?

On a separate sheet of paper, check off these items to make sure you have everything ready for your yard-work business.

☐ Create a budget for your yard-work business.

☐ Draw up a contract for any money you may need to borrow.

☐ Write a list of all supplies you will need. You need to decide if you are using your own tools or using the customers' tools.

☐ Shop for nontool supplies. These might include a hat, sunscreen, water bottle, markers and paper for flyers, and a calendar and notebook for keeping appointments.

☐ Create and distribute advertising flyers.

☐ Organize your schedule and figure out when you can do jobs and how many you can do each day or each week.

☐ Schedule appointments as customers call.

☐ Work hard and enjoy your profits!

If you find you enjoy yard work, you can profit from your new business for many years to come. Seasons, and the yard work that comes with each one, happen over and over again. Are you ready to get to work?

# Glossary

**budget** (BUH-jit)  A plan to spend a certain amount of money in a period of time.

**business plan** (BIZ-nes PLAN)  The "who," "what," "when," "where," and "how" of setting up and running your business.

**contract** (KON-trakt)  An official agreement between two or more people.

**debt** (DET)  Something owed.

**entrepreneurs** (on-truh-pruh-NURZ)  Businesspeople who have started their own business.

**estimating** (ES-teh-mayt-ing)  Making a guess based on knowledge or facts.

**installments** (in-STAHL-ments)  Payment divided into portions to be paid at certain times.

**lump sum** (LUMP SUM)  An amount of money paid all at once.

**profits** (PRAH-fits)  The money a business makes after all its bills are paid.

**slogan** (SLOH-gin)  A word or phrase used in politics or advertising to sell an idea or a goal.

**start-up money** (STAHRT-up MUH-nee)  Money used to start a business.

# Index

# Websites

Due to the changing nature of Internet links, PowerKids Press has developed an online list of websites related to the subject of this book. This site is updated regularly. Please use this link to access the list:
www.powerkidslinks.com/ye/ydwork/